Body Language Secrets:
Total Strangers

D0954700

Body Language Secrets:
Total Strangers

Susan Quilliam

Thorsons
An Imprint of HarperCollins*Publishers*

Thorsons
An Imprint of HarperCollins*Publishers*
77–85 Fulham Palace Road,
Hammersmith, London W6 8JB
1160 Battery Street,
San Francisco, California 94111-1213

Published by Thorsons 1996
10 9 8 7 6 5 4 3 2 1

Susan Quilliam asserts the moral right to
be identified as the author of this work

A catalogue record for this book
is available from the British Library

ISBN 0 7225 3124 9

Printed in Great Britain by
Woolnough Bookbinding Limited, Irthlingborough

To Desmond Morris – who else?

Contents

Acknowledgements

I would first like to acknowledge the many sources and individuals who helped me gain my research material, particularly the staff of the Open University Library, the staff of the University of London Library, and Felicity Sinclair. A special acknowledgement to Samantha Smeraglia for her ability to collate my research so wonderfully!

My thanks also to: Barbara Levy, my agent, for her continued support; to Sharon Scotland, the illustrator; to Jane Graham-Maw, Michele Turney, Jenni Maas and Barbara Vesey from

Thorsons for making the writing and production of this book such an enjoyable experience; to my personal assistant June Bulley for her constant administrative excellence.

A final thank you to my husband Ian who, as always, makes all things possible.

Throughout this book, the people referred to could be either 'he' or 'she'. Consistently referring to one gender would not only raise political issues, but would be unfair to the 'other kind'! In general, therefore, unless to do otherwise would make the text inaccurate, I have alternated pronouns in successive questions in this book, to give a balanced feel.

Preface

Before you read this book, remember that body language:

- is every kind of human behaviour *except* the words spoken – from gestures to breathing, from the way muscles move to a person's use of time
- is not able to tell you everything – you may need the words too
- does not let you read everyone like a book – because everyone has his or her own personalized body language
- will not give you power over people – they will not respond unless they want to

- will not work if you try to change others – you can only ever shift what *you* do and alter the situation that way
- is about gathering information – you will be more successful if you do
- is something you already know – your natural body language works best
- is best tried out slowly and carefully – new body language patterns can look false
- works by trial and error: do more of what succeeds, and stop doing anything that doesn't!

How Can Body Language Help Me When I Am in Public?

The fascination – and the challenge – of public situations is that you are among strangers. Whether in a queue, at a concert, or on a train, everyone around you is in his or her own little world. It is hard to make contact. Whether you enjoy being in public, or feel uneasy, body language can help because it gives you a 'way in'.

If you are interested in other people, then body language gives you an accurate tool to analyse what is going on around you. The nonverbal signals of public spaces and public gatherings are different from private body language, but just as easily interpreted. It is intriguing to watch as people act out public patterns of behaviour, behave differently because they are in a crowd and get drawn into doing things that they would never do alone. And whether you are in a rush or have time to kill, being aware of all this will help you understand human nature just a little more.

You can also use body language in individual interactions. For when you are in public, you are constantly creating relationships with people you do not know and will never meet again – in shops, on buses, in pubs. You can use body language skills to read people's intentions. You can use it to create good relationships with them, however temporary those relationships are. You can use it to block contact with them if that contact feels uncomfortable to you.

In fact, being in public can create dangers that just do not exist when you are on home ground. By using body language to avoid and prevent these situations, where words just are not possible or would not make an impact, you can feel actually be safer. And in the end, if something risky does happen, you can even use body language to escape from it – or to cope with it.

What Is Different About
Body Language in a Shopping Mall?

Public streets, full of tiny shops in the
open air where people and traffic take up
the same space and sometimes have to
compete in order to survive, have created
a very particular body language pattern
– particularly in the colder countries of the
Northern hemisphere.

With the arrival of the mall, the indoor
shopping centre, everything has changed.
Given a roof over our heads, a traffic-free
zone, central heating in the winter and air-
conditioning in the summer, suddenly we have

adopted the shopping body language of
Mediterranean countries.

So, for example, the walking pace of shoppers
in a mall is noticeably slower than on the
street; people stroll rather than hurry. The
architects have supplied walkways five times
as wide as normal pavements, so groups of
several people walk and talk together, rather
than only two abreast at a time. Because of
the lack of traffic, parents are happier for their
children to run ahead, wander to one side, lag
behind. The pace of movement is more
relaxed, more informal, less 'directed'.

We are also more likely to stop in a mall.
There are more seats, less chance of frostbite.
So we will stop to chat, eat a snack, check a
lottery ticket. We will also be more likely to
watch people, for while on the street it is

usually only those with time on their hands –
the old and the young – who sit and stare, in
shopping malls everyone does it. The age
range is much wider, the time spent watching
much longer.

On the other hand, we do not window shop
much in malls. Windows are not as important
as they are on the street, where the only way
to get you inside a shop is to tempt you by a
window display. In the mall, windows are so
unimportant that some shops have removed
them altogether in favour of huge entrance
doors which not only let you see the goods,
but give you direct access to them.

And whereas outdoors, most stores have
automatic doors to keep heating costs down,
in malls the entrances are always open. So
rather than rush from one purchase to

another, in malls we will wander into and out of stores, not really having to make a decision to enter a shop because we do not have to open a door. Sneakily, too, the floor pattern or carpeting of mall shops is designed to look the same as that of the public walkway flooring, to make the distinction between shops and 'street' less noticeable and so tempt you into the shops themselves.

Which is best, street or mall? Because malls are generally more relaxed places to be, they are easier to shop in, more fun – in a word, warmer. But you are more likely to spend more time and more cash there. So, quite literally, you pay your money and you take your choice.

What Is 'Trolley Body Language'?

If a car is an extension of people's personality on the road, then the shopping trolley or cart is the extension of their personality in the supermarket.

Some shoppers are tentative, edging round corners, always hanging back, meeting a 'traffic jam' apologetically and wiggling their way through it; perhaps they are nervous, careful people who lack self-confidence. Then there are the 'ram raiders' who charge through the supermarket banging into other people's trolleys and then simply carrying on; perhaps these are aggressive people, or perhaps they are shopping in their lunch-hour and have a deadline to meet.

The 'park and ride' shoppers place their trolleys at significant points in the shop and then bring their goods back to these central collecting points. They tend to be organized and, if parents, send all the children off on collection duty, to halve the shopping time. Finally, notice the 'kerb crawlers' who hug the side of the frozen food cabinets, poring over the goods; they may be people who have time to shop slowly, or who have to check prices and relative quality before making any decisions.

If two people are in charge of the trolley, problems multiply. They both feel responsible, they both want to feel in control, and that

may make them confrontational. Such trolley wars can occur when one person is pushing but the other keeps hijacking the trolley to different aisles. They can occur when one person is pushing and the other 'lends a hand' unconsciously, slowing the trolley down and altering its direction. And when choosing goods, the trolley can become the battle front line; one person puts something in, the other takes it out, then they stand each side of the trolley and brandish the items across it.

Then comes the checkout. Lone shoppers may display more tension at the checkout than anywhere else, as they try to do everything single-handed – fumble with cheque books, rush their packing, shoot apologetic glances at the people behind them in the queue. Pairs, meanwhile, still find opportunities for conflict – as one is left to unload the trolley while the other goes to get forgotten items; or as one loads the bags while the other hovers at the till and seems to be doing nothing.

How can you personally avoid problems? Watch out for your nonverbal signs of tension: fast, uncoordinated movements; stiff, tense shoulders; white-knuckled hands on the trolley handle. If on your own, slow down and try to shake off any muscle tension. If with a companion, try making physical contact; a pat of your hand or a 'grooming gesture' on the back of your companion's neck can reduce tension instantly. Then divide responsibility – just one person pushing at any one time will guarantee fewer battles. And if you both want control, simply swap roles halfway round the aisles.

How Can I Get Good Service from a Sales Assistant?

When you interact with a sales assistant, you have just a few minutes to create a working relationship and use that to make a successful purchase. In fact, many shop assistants are trained to use body language to support you – but you can help too by using your own nonverbal skills.

As you enter the shop, look for the assistant who has the most effective body language, one who is alert and looks friendly and confident. Steer clear if, as she (or he) interacts with other staff or customers, she looks nonverbally overpushy or completely uninterested. For clothes shopping in particular, you may also want to take the advice of some 'style guides' which suggest that when choosing an assistant you opt for one who has roughly your build and colouring; she will instinctively know, from her knowledge of her own body, what suits you.

Once you have made contact with the most appropriate assistant, put some nonverbal effort into the first few seconds of the interaction. Shop staff so often get treated like a lower form of life that if you make eye contact, smile and pass a comment in a friendly voice, this will immediately relax the assistant and make things more likely to go well.

As you start to look at possible purchases, use your body language to back up rather than to undermine what you are saying. If you want information, for example, use the nonverbal combination of head tilt, questioning smile and raised eyebrows which indicates an interested need to know more; this set of signals is designed to encourage other people to feel good about explaining something.

If you do not want to make a purchase, be clear about that too. It can be tempting to give 'unsure' signals, with your head tilting to one side then the other, a wiggle of your shoulders, a twist of the mouth and hesitation in your voice; somehow these signs seem kinder and less rejecting than a definite no. The problem here is that a trained sales assistant, faced with 'unsure' signals, will automatically try to persuade you. If you are certain you do not want something, and do not want to be pressured, get eye contact, shake your head and use a firm voice.

On the other hand, if the assistant presents you with something you want, then show your appreciation clearly. A thank you, accompanied by a smile of approval, will not only make the assistant delighted that you are pleased but will also lay the groundwork for getting good service next time you enter the store.

What Is 'the Flinch' and How Can It Reduce the Price of a Car?

Salespeople who specialize in big purchases can be intimidating. They depend on your sale for their commission – so they can pressure you to buy on their terms rather than the ones you want. But it does not have to be like this.

Begin by approaching the salesperson confidently. An obviously nervous customer can make a salesperson act even more aggressively, and this is not a good basis for negotiation. Instead, show your willingness to be friendly, with a smile and eye contact, a handshake and an amiable tone of voice.

Create a bond between you that will relax
you both.

Then, take your time to find out about the
product – the different models of car, for
example. Continue to be friendly; you will get
better information and sales service that way.
If you like the product, show this with genuine
smiles, warmth in your voice and nods of
approval – it is a myth that seeming uncertain
about a purchase will cause the salesperson to
lower the price.

But then, as you move towards the sale and
have shown clearly that you really do want
the car or other major item, change your
approach. Remember that salespeople have to
be natural extroverts to succeed in their job.
And extroverts thrive on other people's
friendly approval – but wilt when faced with

disapproval. They will be motivated by pleasing you, urged on by the threat of your displeasure.

So with the sale looming, remove your approval. Let your smile fade, your nods stop, your warm tone disappear. Turn your head slightly away. Frown slightly in disapproval. Shake your head at the price. Let your voice drop in disappointment. In the trade this is known as the 'flinch' – where the customer shows the salesperson that he (or she) has to try that little bit harder. With your friendly body language withdrawn, the salesperson is left feeling bad – and desperately wanting to please you in order to gain the sale.

Then, give him a way to please. Say quite clearly what it is you want – part exchange, a lower price, extended credit. If he is able to provide this, then smile again, put the warmth back into your voice, reach out and give him a congratulatory pat on the shoulder.

If the salesperson is not able to give you what you want, only then do you have to consider whether you are willing to buy anyway. Very often you may decide to do just that – to buy the car, the fridge, or the double glazing at the original price. But flinching is always worth a try. It may work – and if it doesn't, you have lost nothing.

What Really Happens When I Am in the Cinema?

When you go to see a film, you don't simply sit and watch it. In fact, all your body language changes, on the inside as well as on the outside, because without knowing it you are being hypnotized. You may think that hypnosis is some mysterious mental magic, where a stage hypnotist convinces you that you are somewhere else, being someone else. But in fact a hypnotic trance occurs when, focused on one particular thing, you lose track of what is happening in the real world and your body responds by taking on a whole new form of behaviour, externally and internally.

In fact, most of us enter into a mild trance state many times a day – when driving the car, day-dreaming, using a computer. Going to the movies is physiologically just one stage on from this. You are seated in a dark room with no distractions from people, telephones, pets – or the possibility of getting up to make a cup of coffee. In this situation all you have to do is to concentrate on what is in front of you. And in front of you, filling your vision and so filling your mind, are large, bright, moving objects – the images on the screen. Your eyes focus on these, and become so focused that you lose awareness of yourself.

And as you focus so completely, your physiology naturally shifts. You blink less, your breathing rate goes down, your heart rate drops. You are in a different state from normal; a state much more similar to sleep than to being awake – a state of hypnotic trance.

But also, when you are in this state, the film on the screen can affect your body so completely that you almost experience what you see as real. So cinema audiences shift fractionally along with on-screen movement, squaring their shoulders before the big fight, jerking in terror when the monster appears. They do this in synchrony with the screen characters, moving within ¼₈th of a second of their heroes, and in perfect rhythm with them.

And this body language identification is not just on the outside. If you identify with the characters, your internal body language alters too – your muscles, nervous system, heart rate and blood-pressure respond almost as if you were actually in the film yourself. As the hero faces the baddie, your heart rate quickens and your mouth goes dry. As the heroine yearns for her lover, you feel tears coming to your eyes.

For an hour or so you actually believe, mentally and physically, that you are somewhere else, being someone else. You may think you are at the movies. But your body – and your body language – think differently.

How Can Body Language Help Me Get Served in the Pub?

You are standing at the bar in a pub, waiting to be served. The bar staff ignore you. Are you invisible? If so, what can you do? In fact, because of the noise in most pubs, good bar staff get much of their information from nonverbal cues. The secret of getting served in a pub is to realize this and make it work for you.

When you get to the bar, claim your 'territory'. If you do not you may simply get lost in the group of customers who are standing at the bar to drink rather than to order. They will tend to turn sideways or backwards, facing out towards the room. You, on the contrary, should move right up to the bar, rest both elbows on it and face directly inwards to claim your space.

Next, make it clear that you have not been served and want to be. Focus all your attention on the bar person in order to get her (or his) attention. 'Track' her with your body, following her as she moves by turning your shoulders, head and eyes towards her. Do not look away, even for a moment, or you may lose the opportunity to catch her eye. When you do, hold your money visibly in your hand and above bar level, and use that very particular facial expression that both expects and accuses: head tilted on one side, raised eyebrows, closed-mouth smile.

What if you do not get noticed? It is almost certainly because you are using the wrong body language, therefore giving bar staff the wrong information. Turning away from the bar can seem to indicate that you have already been served. Not holding money may give the impression that you want attention but not in order to buy something – so the staff will tend to deprioritize you. Not looking worried may signal that you have not been waiting that long, or that you are not next in the queue; the bar person will turn to someone else.

(Interestingly, in a British pub, the body language of indignation, such as raising your voice, waving your money or screwing up your face in anger, may actually mean staff will ignore you because you are making them feel too pressured!)

How will you know you have been spotted? The bar person will give you eye contact plus one of a number of acknowledgement signals such as a double raised-eyebrow 'flash', a nod or a raised finger. You need to acknowledge this in return with a nod and smile. Then, in fact, as long as you keep facing the bar to signal you are still 'on hold', you can stop trying. Miraculously, when the next drink is served, it will be yours!

What is the Nonverbal Difference between Different Kinds of Restaurants?

When it comes to dining out, there is a sliding scale between low-price places and high-price places. The differences are not only in what you eat and how good the food is, but in the subtle 'scene setting': the nonverbal cues of decor, layout and table arrangement; the body language staff use; the body language you use to them.

Let us start with one of the basics – freedom of movement. You might think that the more you pay, the more liberty you get – but no. At a roadside café or stand, your freedom of

movement is complete – you park where you want, wander across, take your food, disappear into the night. At a motorway service station you are slightly more restricted, funnelled into and out of a food area where several bays offer a choice, but left to your own devices when choosing a table. Compare this with a top-class restaurant, where you are met at the door, marched across to a table chosen for you, seated and largely kept in your place. The aim is so that better-paying customers do not have to move; the result is that your freedom is restricted.

The other result is that the staff themselves move much more in order to deliver the food – and, as a result, move into your personal space. At a low-price eaterie the staff keep well back – behind a counter for self-service, behind a window in a drive-in burger place.

In a medium-level restaurant they come right up to your table with the dishes but then back off and leave you to help yourself. In a 'silver service' establishment, where waiters do everything, they lean round you, across you, between you – moving into your 'intimate' space of 45 cm (18 in) in a way you would normally only allow children and lovers to do!

There is a potential problem here: Human beings feel invaded if unknown people get too close, so the closer service staff are to you, the more threatened you might feel – if they tried to be at all personal. So waiters' nonverbal approach balances out any possible problems. Where staff physically keep their distance, body language can often be quite informal; waiters can smile in a friendly fashion, joke, let their posture and gestures be very familiar, face you directly as an equal. Where staff move close, waiters need to be like wallpaper if they are not to intrude on your evening. So they dress in neutral colours, avoid your line of sight, come up behind you to serve, keep their expressions blank and their voices low and calm.

When you leave, though, the whole relationship shifts. You exit from a burger stand without being noticed. You leave with a minimum of interaction from a pizza place, where the bill is left on your table for you to present at the till in your own time. But the higher the price, the more prolonged and personal the parting. At the Ritz, the waiters present your bill, fetch and carry your credit card, get the receipt, bring your coat, pour you endless 'final' cups of coffee. It is as if, having been so close to you for so many hours, the staff just cannot bear to let you go!

Which Three Agendas Do People Have When They Go Swimming?

Swimming pools are not just for swimming. People have all kinds of reason for going. Next time you are there, watch out for these three agendas ...

Serious swimmers use body language which signals they have a job to do; they are not there for the people. So they will tend to arrive alone, walking briskly in past the turnstiles with a bare smile and nod of greeting at the resident staff. They will find a quiet corner of the changing room – they know just where to go because they are probably here every day. They will change quickly, often having their costumes on under their clothes for speed.

Once in the water they will immediately settle to a regular pace, doing many lengths using the same stroke. They will make hardly any noise. They will never stop to play. They will steer well clear of flumes, wave machines or other distractions. And when resting, or out of the water, they will not look around or approach others. Their lack of expression and eye contact will reveal that they are far more interested in what is going on with their own bodies than with anyone else's – they are concentrating on the sensations of swimming, not on the fun of the pool.

In direct contrast, playful swimmers are only there for the fun. They go in large family or friendship groups, of varying ages and genders, and they will chat, joke, laugh and jostle as they drift up to the turnstiles. In the changing room, they will 'annex' a section of the lockers, taking up a lot of space and often making a lot of noise. Then they will go out as a group into the swimming area and spread over a randomly selected section of 'territory', seats or poolside area.

Playful swimmers will spend almost as much time in the water as serious swimmers, but in a very different way. Their body language will be highly energetic, with lots of movement, noise and touch to show they are close. They will jump, dive or throw things from person to person in the water, but hardly ever swim for more than a few strokes. But, like the serious swimmers, playful swimmers will not gaze around them much. They are not looking to

make new friends; they have enough of their
own.

Then, there are the swimming groupies. These
are almost always young people, and for them
the pool is really a theatre for the teenage
ritual of 'posing and picking up'. They will go
every single day during the school holidays,
until they are old enough to pair off and want
to be alone – after which they may never go
swimming ever again. Groupies, male and
female, will arrive in small, same-sex groups.
They will greet the resident staff like the good
friends they often are, spend time in the
changing room preparing in front of the
mirror, then emerge onto the swimming pool
stage.

Groupies have their own dedicated space,
often near where the staff are based, which

they occupy every day. There they will sit, stand, chat, smile – and 'display' in order to attract attention. Do they look around? Yes, all the time, to check who is watching, to 'accidentally' catch someone's eye. Do they go in the water? Only occasionally, and then usually only when, as an excuse for adolescent loveplay, someone throws someone else in. For this group – except as a backdrop to the fascinating games they are playing – the water itself simply is not important at all!

What Is Interesting About Religious Body Language?

Whether or not you are a believer, the body language of religious worship is fascinating because it reflects such a great deal both about the religion and about the worshippers.

Most religions, for example, suggest that each believer should have a personal religious practice. There will be a recognized body language for this. If the believer needs to worship a deity which is seen as superior, then you will find people kneeling, perhaps with hands joined and pointing towards the heaven

where, in medieval times, the deity was
believed to reside.

Or, if the key act of individual religion is to
repeat and learn sacred scripture, then body
language may help with this, involving an
upright position so that the person can chant
easily, along with some rocking or bowing to
keep a rhythm which helps the worshiper
memorize the relevant verses.

If a central part of one's religious observation
is meditation, with concentration on one's
own body and not outside distractions, then
the body language will include a special
meditation posture. This will probably
involve keeping the spine straight and the
head erect to create a sensation of balance
and calm, closed eyes to shut off outside
input, and some sort of concentration aid

such as a rosary which keeps fingers busy and allows the mind to go free.

Most religions involve group worship – and this too is a nonverbal reflection of belief. In traditional Western, Christian culture, for example, churches have often been built as the biggest, tallest building in a community, designed to show the importance and power of the deity. A church's focus is its altar, with a surrounding area where only celebrants are allowed, and beyond that a larger space for the 'ordinary' congregation. The celebrants – priest, altar boys, choir – dress in splendid costumes which mark them out as special. They will use large, directive gestures which, even from one end of a huge cathedral to the other, show the congregation what to do.

The congregation, obeying these directions,
follow a definite pattern of movement. They
stand – which gives the lungs more breathing
power for singing or praying out loud. They
sit – which allows physical support during a
prolonged sermon. They kneel – again
reflecting the belief in a king-like deity when
praying. Throughout the service, everyone's
body language is controlled, restrained,
respectful and focused on the deity.

But as Christianity has moved towards a
more 'people-centred' approach towards the
end of the twentieth century, body language
has changed to reflect this. So churches may
now be circular to reflect equality among all
people. Celebrants may dress in everyday
clothes, hardly different from those of their
congregation. Services may encourage
spontaneity and freedom of movement. They

may include physical activity such as singing or dancing, not only because it is now realized that such movement gives people a positive feeling physiologically, but also because believers increasingly see human expression as being positive, a reflection of the glory of their god.

And, finally, many services will now include not only an opportunity for direct contact with the deity, through prayer, but also direct contact with the community, with some part of the service incorporating handshakes, kisses or hugs among members of the congregation.

What Is the Basic Body Language of Cars?

Cars may be mechanical objects but they have their own body language, albeit manipulated by their drivers. And, like humans, cars have conscious and unconscious body language – deliberate, controlled, but not necessarily truthful signals, and those signals that reveal the driver's real intentions because they are unconscious and uncontrollable.

A car's conscious body language come from its lights – which of course are specifically designed for 'signalling'. The back lights are there for other road users, indicating a car's movements; through them you get the answers to many questions. Is a car going to stop? – check its brake lights. Is it going to reverse? – See the reversing lights. Is there an emergency ahead? – See the emergency lights flashing on and off. Is the car going to turn left or right? – Look for the indicator lights, which of course are a replacement for the literal body language of a hand waving out of a window.

The front headlights are actually only designed to light up the road ahead for the driver. But they are also used in an informal lights 'language' that is not in the Highway Code, and though not strictly legal, is nevertheless used by many drivers. These lights can show that another car is letting you go first – as when you are turning right and

the car coming towards you flashes its lights.
They are used to say 'Hello!' – as when two
vans from the same firm flash their headlights
as they pass. They are used to tell you there is
a problem – as when you set off at night and
another car 'blinks' to tell you that you have
not switched your lights on. And they are used
to signal that it is safe – as when on a
motorway a lorry flashes to encourage you to
pull in after overtaking (the 'thank you' signal
in return consists of a single flash of your left,
then right, then left rear indicators.)

But all these conscious, controlled driving
signals are often misleading – for a driver can
signal one thing and do something completely
different. The unconscious body language
signs of driving, on the other hand, are the
position of the front wheels. These tell you not
what the driver thinks she is doing, but what

she really is doing – going right, going left, aiming to park, about to do a U-turn. Though the driver is largely unaware of where her front wheels are, they reveal her intentions precisely – even down to when she changes her mind in the middle of a manoeuvre.

So if you really want to understand the body language of a car – more important, if you really want to predict just what a driver is going to do next – watch the car's unconscious rather than its conscious signals!

How Can I Tell When Another Driver Is About to Do Something Dangerous?

Every driver has his own 'safety zone', driving conditions and driving style within which he will drive safely. And it is possible to tell, from the way someone drives, when he is within his safety zone – or whether he is in a situation that is just too demanding for him.

The first possible cue is whether the driver is matching speed to the conditions. Too fast is obviously a problem; 60 miles an hour in traffic in a built-up area will not give anyone time to react within his safety zone, however good a driver he is. But interestingly, driving

too slowly may also indicate that the driver is a potential danger. Driving below the pace of other traffic may indicate that he is nervous or unsure, and so likely to make mistakes.

Driving too close to other cars may mean that a driver is particularly aggressive, or in a hurry – which will make him careless. Too far back, unless he is signalling a manoeuvre, can indicate a timid or sleepy driver.

Another danger signal is if a driver seems to be ignoring road signs. If so, his mental state or the road conditions are probably such that he is not taking in the information he needs to. Beware if a driver straddles the white line, seems to notice a pedestrian crossing only at the last moment, or fails to slow down when he should.

If a driver gives contradictory signals, he may be confused by the road situation. So a car ahead of you indicating left and moving to the right will probably turn right in the end. A car which is slowing down while the driver seems to be looking across to the left is probably about to park, even if the left indicator is not flashing. A car on a roundabout (rotary) that is not signalling at all, but which seems to be sticking to the inner lane, is probably going to come full circle and straight across your bows.

Though most of the body language of driving is actually 'car language', also keep an eye on the 'body' of the driver ahead or the one next to you at the traffic lights. Look out for the driver who continuously turns his head to talk to his passenger, one whose noticeable movements indicate that he is very emotional, one who continuously leans down to change the tape in the cassette player. All these distractions may mean he is unsafe to be near.

In all these situations, you have to decide what to do. Your first line of defence will be the classic one of slowing down slightly and covering the brake. Next, be aware of all the possible manoeuvres the suspect driver might make, and think ahead about what your best response could be.

If the situation seems serious – if you suspect that the driver ahead of you is actually asleep, for example – then your best course of action may well be to turn off and, if you are genuinely concerned about the driver's (and others') safety, get in touch with the police or motorway authorities.

What Is 'Road Rage' and How Can It Kill?

All of us get irritated from time to time, particularly when we are feeling threatened or stressed. Studies of emotion reveal that irritation affects the human body very dramatically. Our whole nervous system goes into action, so that blood rushes to our brain, adrenalin floods our system, our heart rate, breathing and blood-pressure increase; in short, we prepare for action.

If this action does not take place, if we simply ignore the sensations of anger, then we feel very uncomfortable indeed. The most

helpful answer is to reduce the discomfort, perhaps by relaxation or exercise, and then deal calmly with whatever is causing the irritation.

In a car, irritation can build up quite quickly as other people's driving starts to annoy because it threatens us. Particularly if we are in a bad mood to start with – as many people are when they leave the house in the morning to drive to work, or leave work in the evening to drive home – our bodies react speedily with the above-mentioned uncomfortable sensations.

The problem is that in a car we cannot easily reduce our discomfort. We cannot get other people to drive differently. We may not want to stop the car and take some exercise. So the feelings build up. Eventually what we feel is 'road rage'.

When someone drives in a way that restricts or endangers our own progress, we may mutter under our breath or shout obscenities in the direction of the other driver. We may take it further, shaking a fist, putting up two fingers, looking across into the other car with angry, staring eye contact to try to make our point. Road rage can make us want to take even more dramatic action, getting out of our car at the lights, hammering on the other driver's window, even opening the door and attacking her.

Though all of these angry reactions are dangerous, they are not the real killers. Even more dangerous is when we stop expressing our anger through our own body language, and start expressing it through our car's nonverbal signals. If we drive on when we are really angry, then we can put ourselves and others in real danger.

Our vision may narrow, meaning that we do not notice road signs or the manoeuvres of other cars. Our impression of speed may be inaccurate, meaning that we drive faster and carry out manoeuvres at a higher speed. We may misjudge distances, cutting down the space between us and the car in front, or imagining we can squeeze through a gap that is too narrow. We let emotion override our judgement, and therefore start flashing lights, carving people up, even deliberately aiming to nudge other cars, without any real sense of how dangerous this can be.

Because of all this, for our own sakes and everyone else's, it is better to pull over for a few minutes and strangle a lamp-post rather than simply carry on driving when we feel 'road rage'.

How Can I Cope with Officials?

There is a certain kind of body language which officials are trained to use. And if you are dealing with ticket inspectors, police officers and traffic wardens, then it is as well first to understand these very particular nonverbal cues, and then be able to cope with them.

The mark of authority figures is often the uniform they wear, which echoes military power and status. So doormen and ward matrons alike often wear dark uniforms, in black, blue or green, with metal badges and a helmet or cap that not only gives an impression of formality but also adds height.

Along with all this, authority figures usually develop status body language. They will stand or sit erect, their shoulders back and with a set, slightly expressionless face. They will avoid uncontrolled gestures, signals of friendship such as broad smiles, and slightly quirky behaviour such as a wink or a giggle. Their voices will be steady and strong, their tone formal and polite.

In response to all this, even in situations where we are not under threat in any way, many of us do become nervous. Somehow, faced with all these body language signals of power and status, we start to feel inferior or even slightly guilty. We may look down submissively, start stuttering or stammering, make little 'escape movements' with our hands or feet, and bite our lips as if to stop ourselves saying something we might regret. One study showed that at the approach of a police officer, both women and men used protective gestures – arms across the body or hands instinctively moving to protect the crotch!

Instead of becoming nervous when faced with authority like this – whether stopped by a ticket inspector or faced with a traffic warden – the key is to keep calm. You need, of course, to show in your body language that you acknowledge the presence of authority, so you may choose not to stare directly at the official, leap up in a confrontational way, or talk in a loud and argumentative tone. But equally, it is as well not to seem so nervous that you arouse suspicion, nor so friendly that you seem to be trying to distract the official from the matter in hand.

Instead, relax as much you can. Breathe slowly and steadily to allow your body to calm down. Stay seated unless asked to get up, then stand easily with your head slightly tilted so as not to seem challenging. Keep a pleasant expression and answer any questions in an untroubled but not jokey tone of voice.

Finally, when your ticket is clipped or your driving licence checked to the official's satisfaction, you may notice a mental 'signing off' process. You are obviously not a danger, so the body language of authority relaxes just slightly. In response, you can also be more at ease – though not too much more – acting just slightly more informal to reflect the fact that although this is an authority figure, he now realizes that he does not need to assert his authority over you.

Why Do People Set Up Home Every Time They Travel on a Train?

Human beings like the security of knowing that they have their own space – even in situations where, in fact, everything is public property. Look at passengers on a train. If the journey is to be a relatively long one, there is more need to have a safe 'home base'. Acknowledging this, train designers have provided four-seat bays which lend themselves very easily to the creation of little territories.

Watch, then, for passengers 'house-hunting'. They may already have formally reserved their space; but if not, they will walk down the

train, outside or inside, choosing a spot that
fulfils their needs. Is the bay facing the engine,
is it near the buffet, near the toilet, is it
smoking or non-smoking? Is it a two-seater
bay, which gives more privacy but less space,
or a four-seater where someone else will come
along to share? Once chosen, 'territory' will
be marked: coat on luggage rack, bag on seat
and something on the table to make absolutely
sure that no one intrudes.

If passengers who know each other are
sharing a bay, they will feel able to spread out
across the table. But if strangers are sharing,
there will be a nonverbal negotiation about
territory not only on but also under the table.
Both passengers shift papers, move food and
drink, cross and uncross legs – all to the
accompaniment of sideways glances and
reassuring smiles – until both are satisfied that

they have what they need. This could be that each person gives up all the room because he or she does not want it – or it could be that there is a mental dotted line down the middle of the table that marks the division between each person's space.

And within that space, passengers will actually feel able to do many of the things that they do at home. They will eat. They will sleep. They will read. If a group is sitting together, they will talk, play games, drink beer. They will apply makeup and do their hair. They will work on business papers, use a calculator, talk into a portable phone, type into a computer.

It is not just that there is space for all these activities – the leg room provided is similar to that on an underground train. It is not just that there is a table provided – restaurants have these but diners do not annex them in quite the same way. It is that, insecure in the way only travellers can be, passengers need to feel they have a place which, even for just the few hours they are travelling, is Home Sweet Home.

How Do People Use Body Language to Survive on a Rush-hour Tube Train?

On the London Underground, people are regularly, consistently, inexorably pressed up against other people every day. So it is not surprising that Tube commuters, like all humans in crowded and static situations, use a particular set of nonverbal strategies simply in order to survive.

The natural human response to strangers is to keep our distance. But in a crowded train carriage, we simply cannot. So we have to protect ourselves: We put up barriers, using shoulder bags and brief cases held in front of

our bodies or, failing that, using crossed arms
or hands held at crotch height. We read
newspapers and magazines to prevent eye
contact with others; if there is room, we open
our papers out so that we can hide behind
them even further. We hunch our shoulders as
if not hearing what is going on around us. So
as not to invite approaches we will seem
unapproachable, staring through people,
keeping our expressions blank and unsmiling,
making no contact at all.

As well as to give self-protection, Tube body
language has also developed to indicate that we
are not threatening to other people. So we take
up as little space as possible, tucking in elbows
and bags so as not to make contact, bowing our
heads slightly in the age-old submissive
movement that tells other people we are not
going to make trouble. When new people enter

the carriage, we shift slightly, as if to make room for them, even if in actual fact there is nowhere to shift to. If we have to press up against someone, then we shrug and smile apologetically as if to say that it is not really our fault.

All these behaviours work quite well – until things get just too much. It is a hot day, just one too many squeezes in past the sliding doors, and all of a sudden the body language alters. We become nervous, turning this way and that as if looking for a way out. We finger our collars as if trying to breathe more easily. We start to fidget, making little 'escape movements' with our fingers in place of the running movements we really want to make with our feet.

Happily, it usually all stops there, as at the next station the carriage empties somewhat – and our body language moves back to normal again.

How Do Airports Use Nonverbal Cues to Make Life Easier?

Consider the challenge that airports face: Every day, hundreds of thousands of passengers need to be channelled from the checkout desks where they arrive, through to the planes on which they depart. How can that best happen? The secret is in creating the right environment, one that nonverbally guides yet also reassures.

You arrive at an airport. You may be nervous; studies reveal that air travellers perform ten times more anxiety gestures, such as rechecking tickets, than train travellers do.

You will probably head straight for the
check-in desks. There, you are greeted by a
member of the airline staff who gives you
body language signals that combine two
things: efficiency (an authoritative uniform,
formal language and directive gestures) and
friendliness (direct eye contact and a broad
smile). The aim of this combination is to make
you feel first secure and then calm – maybe
airport staff do not want you panicking before
or during the flight.

The check-in desks not only make you feel
safe. They also relieve you of your baggage,
which means that you can move about easily.
This is a practical strategy, and one that also
means that you are not tempted to wander
away from the airport – which now has your
belongings – and so delay your flight. You are
freed up to wander round. You have certainly

got time to do this; your pre-flight nerves,
along with your pre-flight instructions, mean
that you may well have arrived anything up to
two and a half hours before your plane takes
off.

During that two and a half hours, what are
you likely to do, in your anxious state? You
will want to eat (humans often eat to steady
their nerves), and you may want to buy all the
things that you think you may have forgotten
(another documented reaction to anxiety).
And guess what? – Airports deliberately
provide ample opportunities to eat and shop
– and, outside the departure lounge at any
rate, not much opportunity simply to sit and
wait. Sneaky, huh?

After a while, however, airports become keen
to divide off people who are travelling from

those in the airport for other reasons. They want to complete the time-consuming pre-flight checks – such as security and passport control – just in case something goes wrong. They want to move you a little nearer to your flight, so that you will be more likely to be in the right place at the right time. So they call you, well in advance, into the departure lounge. This is smaller, not only because fewer people use it, but also because it is not so filled with shops which might make it likely that you would miss the call to your gate.

When you are called to the boarding gate, you become part of an even more tightly specified group – this time, of passengers who are flying on a particular plane. You are placed in a separate lounge where you have absolutely nothing to do – so that when you are finally allowed to board, no one has the slightest excuse to be distracted, and no one goes missing at the last moment.

Finally, you hand in your boarding pass and walk onto the plane. And at this point, the airport staff heave a sigh of relief. Their nonverbal strategies have succeeded in getting you successfully on the plane and off their hands. Happy landing!

What Is the Body Language of Queuing?

The body language of queuing has really only developed since the Second World War. Before that, people simply gathered in a random way at bus stops or in shop doorways. Then when a bus arrived or a shop opened, they stepped forward in any order. This rather casual attitude to taking your turn came not only from a much more leisurely lifestyle, but also from a belief that there was enough for everybody. Rationing and the war changed that belief – now, queuing is a part of life.

The classic post-war 'line' queue happens when people spontaneously stand one behind another. It is usually found in shops and supermarkets; people stand strictly in place, slightly closer than they normally would to a stranger, as if to make the queue look shorter. You will see irritated movements if someone at the front of the queue takes longer than the average time for his transaction. But people will rarely talk because they are too busy checking their own queue to see how fast it is moving, too busy looking around at other queues to see if it is worthwhile 'swapping'. If it is, there will be a sudden flurry of activity, as some people swap, others debate whether to swap, and yet others start to swap and then stay where they are.

The 'funnelled' queue is a recent development. It is found in service buildings such as banks and libraries, and consists of a series of waist-high tapes which first guide you into a single queue, then direct you from there to a number of service points. Body language here is different from the classic queue because there is little possibility of speeding up the process, or of competing for a place in other queues. So people in funnelled queues are in general much less tense. They do not need to keep a watching eye out, so they will talk much more, and in a much more informal way. They will be more co-operative – pointing out to the person in front that it is his turn to be served; helping others move prams or shopping baskets forward.

Recently, there has been a return to prewar days, with far more 'random queues', particularly in outdoor situations such as at bus stops. Here, new arrivals look round at others to check who is there before them and to signal to others that they know their place in the queue – in supermarkets this process is often controlled by giving you a ticket to mark your place in, for example, the delicatessen line. Once someone has given this 'look around' signal, he can move about quite casually, wandering quite far away from the bus stop without losing his 'place'.

When the bus arrives, if there are seats for all, people move forward slowly and calmly with no real concern for who goes first. But if there are only a few places, then suddenly everything changes. People will rush to the front if they were there first or are desperate for a place; they will hang back if they feel that they came sufficiently late not to be likely to get a place; they will tackle queue-jumpers severely with sharp elbows and an angry tone of voice.

Then, as the bus fills up and drives away,
anyone left behind to wait for the next one
calms down – and once again people scatter
randomly about until the next bus comes.

What Can I Do to Make Sure
I Do Not Get into a Fight in Public?

The first step in avoiding a fight is spotting the problem before it starts. Be wary, for example, of any situation where alcohol is flowing, as this increases aggression. Be wary too of an overheated environment, such as a crowded pub or disco; when temperatures rise, so do tempers.

Watch out too for body language that tells you when people are likely to be dangerous. Alarm bells should ring if others seem to be using provocative body language. They may take on a strutting walk, square their

shoulders, look around at possible
competitors with a firm gaze that locks eye
contact. These are all nonverbal signals that
naturally appear just as a fight starts. By using
them beforehand, without reason, people who
want a fight invite violence – and the unlucky
person who ends up on the floor will be the
one who returns or responds to these signals.
If you want to avoid being so unlucky, turn
slightly away, relax your shoulders, avoid eye
contact, simply ignore the invitation.

What if the possibility of a fight comes
unannounced? You are in the middle of a
conversation and suddenly realize that things
are getting physical. You may notice the
signals mentioned above, but this time they
will be more pronounced because they are
more personal. Watch out too for gestures
that show someone is ready for action, such as

arms held away from the body or fists clenching and unclenching. Be prepared for signs that your opponent's body is ready for activity, such as increased breathing, sweating, a reddening of the skin. Be particularly wary of sudden paleness – which is a sure sign that the body is on the point of action.

The most useful thing to do at this stage is to use the body language of non-confrontation. Of course, you may feel that you have to attack on principle – and if you want to, then go ahead. You may think that the body language of non-confrontation is the same as that of nervousness – and if you do, then you will be in for a shock, as these signals will encourage the other person to bully you.

Instead, try true non-confrontational body language. If you are heading for a fight and want to avoid it, then studies have shown that if you simply reduce your height compared to that of your opponent, this will signal that you are not up for a fight and remove much of the aggression from the situation. Slump your shoulders, bow your head, drop your eyes. Looking deeply into your beer or tying your shoelace would do the trick.

Stay in this position until your opponent has found someone else to pick on. Then, walk quietly and unobtrusively away.

What Can I Do to Make Sure
I Do Not Get Mugged or Molested?

As with steering clear of a fight, avoiding muggers and molesters is firstly about being alert to the danger signs. But then, because criminals like an easy life, rather than back down you need to make it look as if attacking you would be more trouble than it is worth.

The first nonverbal danger signal may be a risky place. Steer clear of dark, deserted areas, with plenty of spots for people to hide, such as lonely lanes and parks after dark. Bear in mind, though that unfortunately some of the worst attacks happen in broad daylight near public places.

The second danger signal may be risky people.
You cannot judge from appearance – some
muggers are among the best-dressed people in
town. But alarm bells should ring when you
are on your own and people approach you
without the body language that is normally
used when approaching a stranger in the street
– coming from behind rather than face to face,
speeding up rather than slowing down as they
come close.

Can you avoid being approached like this?
The bottom line is that a mugger will choose
to attack someone who looks as if he (or she)
will give in easily. Any nonverbal signs of fear
act as a fuel to violence; even big, strong
people can be victims if their body language
signals that they are. So do not walk with
your head down, shoulders slumped,
slouching, or making nervous side-to-side eye

movements. Instead, however wary you may feel, keep your head up, your gaze up, your movements alert. Look as if you would actually be able to fight back if you were attacked – clench your fists if that is what it takes to look and feel aggressively confident.

If you do feel that you are under threat, then take action that keeps you in control. If you hear footsteps behind you, walk with longer strides and more quickly, but do not break into a nervous run. Cross the road so that you have a chance to see behind you. Head straight for where there are most people – preferably a main road, but up the path of a lighted house if are absolutely desperate.

If someone comes up to you, again stay in control. If you are seated, perhaps at a bus stop or on a station platform, get up and face your attacker. If standing, stand tall. Put a barrier such as a bench or chair between you if at all possible; if nothing is available, use a bag or briefcase held in front of you. Try to look bigger, squaring your shoulders and breathing in to enlarge your chest. Lock your gaze with that of your attacker. And however much you may feel that you might be able to talk your attacker round, do not smile, touch or enter into conversation; these things will provide a lever with which to control you. Instead, say in a loud, low firm voice 'Go away – now ...' Then make as much noise as you can to attract attention and help.

Remember that attackers want easy prey. If you can convince them that you are not it, they may well go away.

What Body Language Is Worth Noticing during a Team Event?

As a spectator it is interesting to watch how the body language of a team slowly shifts throughout a game – as they gradually start to lose, or head for a win.

As the teams run on at the start of the game, they will signal just how nervous they are. Do they look serious or worried, use fiddly gestures to adjust kit and equipment, make eye contact only with each other but not with the crowd or the opposing team? If they do, then they are anxious.

Some players and coaches will be using body language 'rituals' to reduce that nervousness and create team spirit – chants, clapping, stamping feet. These work largely by making each team member 'match' or parallel the body language of the others, so that they not only feel closer but are also more likely to predict what team members are going to do and be able to respond successfully to it.

The contest starts. Of course, there will be setbacks for both sides. And some players will respond to these setbacks by using body language that is less effective: losing energy, becoming less co-ordinated, seeming less able to respond to other team members, throwing fits of temper. Other players will use setbacks to spur them on: becoming more energetic, moving faster, responding more accurately to team-mates, 'matching' others more.

In some games, a seeming setback can be
turned to advantage – by using deceitful body
language. If fouled, a player may start to
exaggerate all the signs of injury and distress.
Curling up, rolling over, bowing the head and
screwing up the face all act as an unspoken
appeal to the referee to take revenge on behalf
of the player. Mysteriously, if the player is
genuinely injured, you will rarely see any of
these signs because they are not needed – and,
of course, once the incident is over, these
signals disappear within seconds!

When a point is scored, a successful team will
celebrate. They will suddenly find a spurt of
energy, so will run, leap, kick, punch the air.
And, particularly in a very physical sport, they
will probably touch, a very basic way humans
have of celebrating. The team who has just
lost a point, on the other hand, will run back

to their places with heads down, without making eye contact, without touching – and will tend not to react with aggression at this point, almost as if attacking behaviour is only relevant when they are in the lead, or at least on equal terms. If they are losing, even if only temporarily, they dare not actively attack.

At the point that it becomes obvious that one team will win, each team will also display totally different nonverbal cues. The losers will be quiet, passive, solitary as they walk off the field. The winners, on the other hand, will be euphoric. They will crowd together, smiling, laughing, touching. The changing room and the showers will be full of energetic body language, noise and horseplay – as if now work is over, the team is reverting to childhood body language as they play for a while.

How Might I 'Go Mad' – and How Can I Keep Sane – in a Big Crowd?

Being with a big and active crowd – at a concert, say – can feel very good. If you feel safe, and particularly if you have something in common with all the other people, then the fact of being in close contact can excite you. If people are moving, singing or shouting rhythmically, then you can join in; 'matching' or copying movement is a positive experience for humans. You may turn to other people and talk to them, make physical contact with them by dancing together, touching or hugging. You feel close to them, united.

So far, so good. But in a crowd there may be just too much going on. There are too many people, with too many voices, too much noise and too much interaction. While this kind of interaction is stimulating, your body can go into overload – with the result that you may start to feel aggressive. Studies show that overcrowding leads our bodies to produce too much adrenalin, which can make us feel violent. And then, given that being in a crowd also leads to a sense of irresponsibility, it can be easy to find something to do with this violence. And very soon, there is the concert stampede, the football riot – and the lynch mob.

If you are in a crowd and start to feel that something is going wrong, then your first line of defence is to leave, at least for a short while. Just stepping off the dance floor or going for a walk can calm your nervous system down, make you feel less aggressive, get you more in touch with your natural sanity.

But what if you cannot leave? Edging your way out of a football crowd can be impossible, particularly if you want to see the whole of the game. A quick way of avoiding the insanity factor, is to prevent yourself getting affected by the crowd. Stop moving with those around you, singing with them, shouting with them. Turn to one individual person near you, make eye contact with her (or him) and smile to make the interaction more personal. If necessary, take a break from the input by putting your hands over your ears and shutting your eyes. Calm yourself by taking deep breaths.

This may only be a temporary measure, but it can make being in a crowd a sane – rather than an insane – experience.

How Can I Make Love in Public?

It sounds outrageous. Of course you would not dream of actually making love in a crowd. But, in fact, people often do get much more physically intimate in public spots than they would do anywhere else except at home alone. They will kiss, cuddle – and more – in front of thousands of strangers in a way they would not in front of two or three friends. Why?

A key reason is that being in an anonymous group of people – in the middle of the shopping centre as well as in the back row at the movies – does alter human body language.

You may feel as if you can do more and not be noticed. This happens because members of a crowd of human beings tend not to make eye contact with those they pass; such a personal link feels far too threatening. And so because when people look around at the mass of humanity no one makes eye contact, the impression people get is that they cannot be seen. It seems as if you can do anything and not be noticed.

Also, when you are with a partner in a crowd, you automatically use body language that blocks you off from other people and creates a little world of your own. You position yourself so that you are less likely to be noticed – such as on that infamous 'back row'. You stand so that the taller one of you has his or her back to the crowd and shields the other from people's gaze. You lean into each other, face to face, eye to eye. And you build little 'tents' of clothing, so that hugs happen under the protection of two open jackets, and intimate touches take place under the protection of a coat spread across a lap.

This kind of protection and anonymity gives you the opportunity to be intimate. And it also gives you the motivation: Touching, cuddling, kissing are fun, and knowing that you are in a slightly risky situation, among all these people – even if they do not seem to be looking – adds that extra frisson. The slight fear raises your heart rate, gets your adrenalin going, makes your body more sensitive. Being in public arouses you. It feels good – so you do it.

What Is the Secret of Success When Speaking in Public?

The difference between being someone who speaks well in public and one who does not is not in the words you say. The secret of successful public speaking is much more in *how* you say those words.

Good public speakers grab the audience's attention the minute they take the floor. Their walk to the podium, or their rising to speak, are all part of the performance. So as you make your entrance walk tall, stand straight, seem confident by holding your head high, however nervous you are. Look round and

make eye contact with individuals in all parts of the room.

As you begin to speak, check your posture. If you stand with your weight on one side or sit with your legs crossed, you will seem to the audience to be physically off-balance, even mentally uncertain of what you are saying. If you bend over the podium or clutch your notes on your lap, you will seem nervous and insecure. Instead, whether seated or standing, get firmly balanced, with both feet on the floor.

Use your eyes. Look up and out to the audience as much as you can; this is one reason for using minimal notes and not reading what you are going to say. Do visual 'sweeps' of the room, looking to the back left, back right, front left, front right as you speak.

Then let your gaze linger on just one or two individuals in the audience and make particular contact. That way, everyone in the audience will feel that you are talking directly to her or him, and will listen intently to what you say.

Voice is obviously all important. If there is no microphone, raise the pitch of your voice slightly rather than the volume to make sure that you can be heard. Concentrate on variety, altering your speed and rhythm, allowing your voice to rise with emotion and then drop, taking a 'dramatic' pause – all these can keep the audience's interest where a flat, monotone delivery will make them fall asleep.

Also use your gestures to help you. There is no need to wave your hands like flags – but remember that gestures add emphasis, generate interest, create mood. Use a direct, downwards 'baton' gesture to stress a particularly important word or phrase. Use a wide, arms-open inclusive gesture when you want your audience to agree with what you are saying. And if your speech contains emotion, then allow yourself to let your hands reflect this, perhaps clenching your fist or clasping both hands together to show how strongly you feel.

As you begin to move to the end of your speech, do not 'fade away' nonverbally. It may be tempting to rush through the last words and exit as quickly as you can. But this can leave the audience feeling as if your speech has been inconclusive. Instead, slow down, keep your voice strong, keep looking at your listeners, and end with an open-handed 'It is your turn now' gesture and a smile. This way, you are not only signalling that you are about to finish speaking; you are not only signalling that you want your audience's attention right to the last word; you are also signalling that you expect a response from your audience – and a positive response at that.

What Can I Learn by Watching Body Language on the Beach?

If you want the time, the opportunity and the leisure to see body language in all its many forms, take a beach holiday. On the beach you will see almost every kind of nonverbal communication there is: individual, groups, crowds; men, women, children; people flirting, bonding, child-rearing. There is much too much to describe – but here are a few interesting patterns to look for.

As people arrive, watch them mark out their 'territory'. They will spread out towels, put up umbrellas, loungers, windbreakers and even

BODY
LANGUAGE
SPOTTERS
GUIDE

tents – all to claim their spot. They will then decide just where the boundaries are – and very often pace them out. On a crowded beach, territory will extend only as far as the edge of the towel, while on a more deserted beach a group might mark out a strip of territory between them and the sea, and guard it by a constant stream of trips to the water's edge. If another group intrudes, the first group will give hostility signals, glancing across, murmuring among themselves, invading in return by letting a ball or a dog 'accidentally' stray into the other group's space.

As people begin to feel comfortable on their territory, they will start to undress. Beaches, in fact, offer the best displays of public nudity you will ever see. You can tell those whose first day it is on the beach not only by their colour, but also by how slowly they disrobe.

By two or three days into their holiday they will not only have got their favourite 'territory' but will be happy to take their clothes off within minutes of settling down. You can, incidentally, often tell just which body part – chest, breast, bum, tum or thighs – each sun-worshiper is most insecure about, because it will be the last one he or she reveals.

Because of this partial nudity – and the inhibitions it places on people – you will rarely see full sexual body language on the beach. But, holidays being what they are, you will see lots of romance. So singles will 'display' their best points in the hope of attracting a mate: women will stretch out long legs and toss their hair back; men will broaden their shoulders and show off their physique by swimming and playing beach games.

Already-existing couples will use body
language that shows how very close they are,
'matching' or copying each other's posture,
spontaneously lying or sitting in the same
way. Watch as they put sun tan lotion on each
other: the extent to which each partner is
happy to spread it and comfortable about
receiving it will be a clear indication of just
how far their physical relationship has gone!

Couples with families may occasionally be
romantic with each other, but their body
language is much more likely to be focused
around their children. You can tell by looking
just which child is the most trouble – the one
that parents compulsively watch. Which child
is a bit of a loner? – That will be the one
playing far away, with her back turned
unconcernedly to the family group. Which
child is unhappy or a bit unpopular? – The

one who clings to his parents, or who plays alone but with constant glances over at the family group.

So, as you lie back in the sun and slap lotion on all over, put down your blockbuster novel for a while and look around. All human body language is there ...